BABOONS

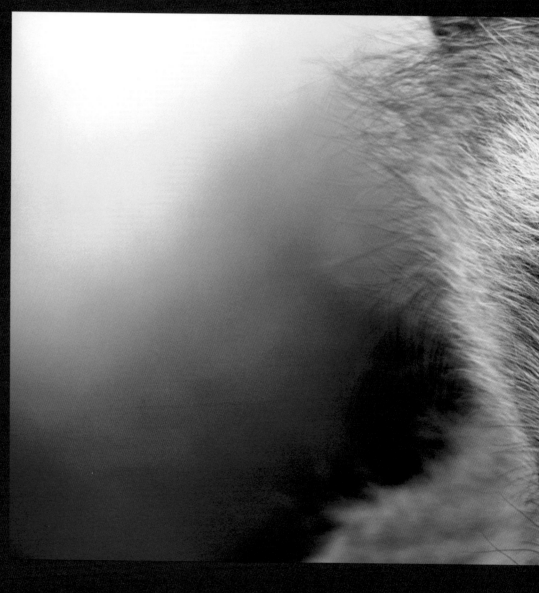

by Sophie Lockwood

Content Adviser: Barbara E. Brown, Associate, Mammal Division, The Field Museum, Chicago, IL

THE CHILD'S WORLD®, CHANHASSEN, MINNESOTA

BABOONS

Published in the United States of America by The Child's World®
PO Box 326 • Chanhassen, MN 55317-0326 • 800-599-READ • www.childsworld.com

Acknowledgements:

The Child's World®: Mary Berendes, Publishing Director

Editorial Directions, Inc.: E. Russell Primm, Editorial Director; Pam Rosenberg, Editor; Judith Shiffer, Assistant Editor; Matt Messbarger, Editorial Assistant; Susan Hindman, Copy Editor; Emily Dolbear, Proofreader; Judith Frisbie and Olivia Nellums, Fact Checkers; Tim Griffin/IndexServ, Indexer; Cian Loughlin O'Day, Photo Researcher, Linda S. Koutris, Photo Editor

The Design Lab: Kathleen Petelinsek, Designer, Production Artist, and Cartographer

Photos:

Cover/frontispiece: Paul A. Souders/Corbis; half title: Kennan Ward; CIP: Digital Vision.

Interior: Animals Animals/Earth Scenes: 8 (D. Allen Photography), 12 (Ingrid Van Der Berg), 16 (Manoj Shah), 29 (Robert Winslow); Corbis: 5-middle left and 22 (Wolfgang Kaehler), 21 (Brian A. Vikander); Digital Vision: 5-top left and 11, 25; Gallo Images/Corbis: 27 (Daryl Balfour), 32 (Martin Harvey); Getty Images/The Image Bank/Joseph Van Os: 5-bottom right and 30, 19; Photodisc: 5-top right and 15; Reuters/Corbis: 5-bottom left and 36 (Alexandra Winkler), 34 (Gleb Garanich).

Library of Congress Cataloging-in-Publication Data

Lockwood, Sophie.
  Baboons / by Sophie Lockwood.
      p. cm. — (The world of mammals)
  Includes index.
  ISBN 1-59296-497-4 (lib. bdg. : alk. paper) 1. Baboons—Juvenile literature. I. Title.
II. World of mammals (Chanhassen, Minn.)
  QL737.P93L63 2005
  599.8'65—dc22   2005000533

TABLE OF CONTENTS

Chapter One

Crop Raiders

It was the worst news the South African research team could hear. The Chacma baboon **troop** they had studied for four years had started raiding farmers' crops. The scientists had always known the problem might come up. The long rains that nourished the **savanna** had not come this year. Water holes dried up. Trees produced little fruit. Grasses withered on the plains. The hungry monkeys looked for food wherever they could find it. A neighboring field full of corn provided a delicious change from the dismal savanna plant life.

Not surprisingly, the farmer was not happy about the baboons eating his corn, and the animals' lives were in danger. Some humans think of baboons as **vermin**—the rats of the monkey world. Raiding baboons are shot on sight. The scientists wanted to move the monkeys to a new territory. The trouble was finding a place for them to live. National parks weren't an option because they already had too

Would You Believe?
Baboons are monkeys. The easiest way to tell a monkey from an ape is by the tail. Most monkeys have tails, and apes do not.

Baboons are found in many countries of Africa south of the Sahara Desert.

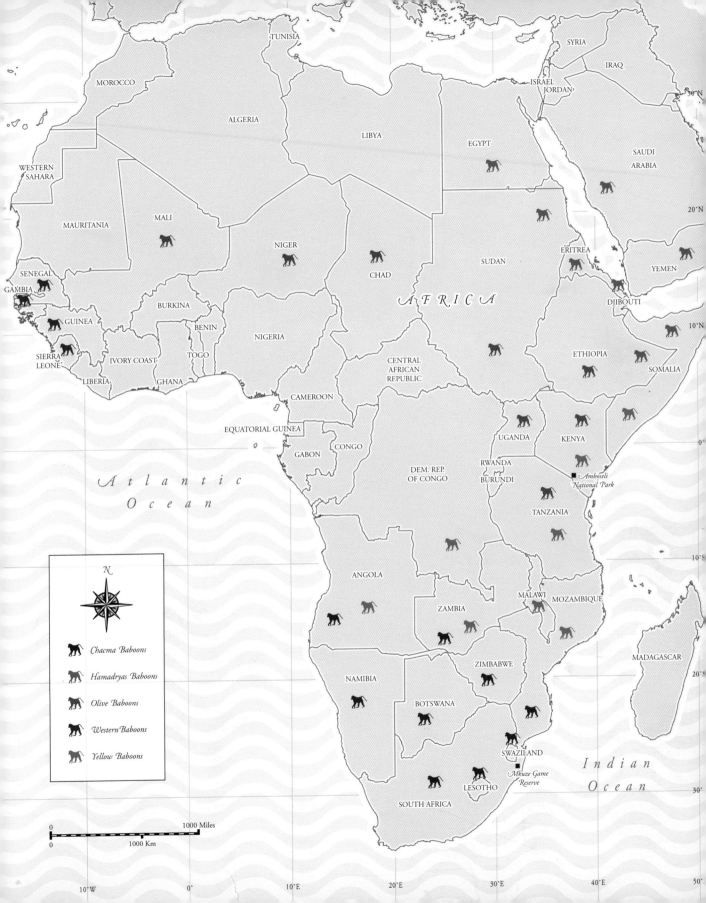

many baboons. The scientists asked ranch owners and local tribes. Most said, "No!"

Finally, the team found the perfect site. Steep cliffs where the troop could sleep rose on both sides of a rock-strewn, grassy canyon. A natural spring not too far away provided fresh water. Acacia and fig trees dotted

Common names for the Chacma baboon include dog-faced monkey and savanna baboon.

the savanna. The place offered a sleeping site, water, and food. The land was too rocky for cattle to graze or crops to grow, which made it easy to convince the landowner.

Next, scientists planned the move. They had to capture, transport, and release forty-two baboons. Most baboons are smart and hard to trap. Chacma baboons are a large savanna baboon **species.** Males can weigh as much as 27 kilograms (60 pounds). Cages needed to be roomy and strong.

The scientists put fifty open cages near the baboons' sleeping site. They used extra cages to help make sure all the baboons were captured. Researchers wired the cage doors open and placed food inside. The animals quickly got used to the cages. **Juvenile** baboons played on them like human children play on playground equipment.

After three days, the scientists set the spring-loaded doors. When a baboon took the food in a cage, the door would drop shut. At least, that was the plan.

Baboons feed in the daytime. Early in the morning, the juveniles climbed down from the trees to feed. They entered the cages, and *slam!*— the doors shut. The scientists worried that the other monkeys would be wary of the cages once some troop members were

Would You Believe?
When a baboon can't find its troop, it shouts, "Wahoo, wahoo!" Other baboons quickly answer, and the lost monkey finds its way.

caught. Hunger won out over caution. Within two hours, all but one baboon was caged.

The holdout was Denu, a **dominant** adult male. Denu was the most clever baboon in the troop. He had figured out how to steal the food out of the cages without getting trapped. The scientists tried darting Denu with sleeping potions. Denu stayed just beyond the darts' reach. He stared down his thin **muzzle** with his close-set dark eyes. Finally, the researchers tricked Denu with a taste treat he could not resist—bananas. The trapdoor closed, and the researchers loaded the trucks for the big move.

The baboons shrieked. They didn't know what was happening, and they were frightened. The scientists blocked the sides of the trucks so that the baboons could not see where they were going. That way, the baboons wouldn't be able to head back to their original home.

Arriving at the canyon site, the team quickly unloaded the cages. They released juveniles and females with infants first. The monkeys rocketed out of the cages and into the dense grass. Next, the **adolescents** left their cages, calling out, "Wahoo, wahoo." Answering grunts gave the young baboons a direction to follow. The scientists released the dominant males last.

Would You Believe?
Baboons are as individual as humans. They have different appearances and personalities. In fact, scientists studying baboon troops often name each monkey. Sometimes, relatives are given names that begin with the same letter. For example, Mary, a female Chacma baboon, might have young named Mila, Molly, and Mick.

They, too, called "Wahoo, wahoo" and hurried to join the troop.

In the morning, the troop climbed down from their rocky sleeping site. They formed small groups for **foraging.** The adult females found star grass, a food they recognized from their old territory. Denu climbed a fig tree and tried the fruit. This was a new treat, with a pleasant, sweet flavor. He soon had company, and the baboons happily plucked ripe figs from the branches.

Baboons spend most of their time on the ground, but they climb trees to find food, to escape predators, and to sleep.

The baboons needed to find their new water source. The scientists had to lead them away from the feeding area to the water hole. They left a trail of bananas from the base of the cliff where they slept to the water. A dominant female, Lucy, was curious enough to enter strange territory and find the water hole. She led the troop to the pool. They ringed the water's edge, drinking, with their bottoms in the air.

Chacma baboons at Mkuze Game Reserve in South Africa stop for a drink of water.

Chapter Two

Just Like Humans

Baboon troops can have as few as 10 and as many as 200 (and occasionally more) monkeys. Think of a troop like an apartment building. Many people of varying ages live in the same place. They are not all related to each other, but they share common bonds.

A baboon troop also shares common bonds. The baboons find food and drink together. Dominant males work together to defend the troop. Adult females and males share child care duties. Within the troop, some monkeys have close ties and friendships.

Baboons pass through different stages of life, just like humans. A single infant is born (baboon twins are rare). A newborn baboon weighs about 1 kilogram (2 lbs). An infant grips its mother's fur tightly. As the mother forages for food, baby rides against her belly. The infant sucks milk from its mother's nipple as mom feeds. For the next few weeks, the baby clings to its mother.

At one month old, a baboon infant begins to climb about. The infant still spends most of its time with its mom,

sleeping at night in her arms. At three or four months, the baby begins to eat solid foods. This is much like human development—except a four-month-old baboon eats berries, flowers, and grass, not strained applesauce. The infant continues to drink milk from its mother until it is almost a year old.

JUVENILES AND ADOLESCENTS

By the time a baboon reaches the "terrible twos," it usually has a new brother or sister. During the day, juveniles play with other young baboons, forage for food, and explore. They usually sleep near their mothers each night.

Young baboons chase each other, swing in trees, and wrestle. When faced with something strange or threatening, they make a noise that sounds like "geck, geck, geck." Gecking means "I'm afraid."

Female juveniles bond closely with their mothers, sisters, and other female cousins. There is a pecking order in baboon troops. A strong, dominant female holds a high rank. Her daughters and granddaughters will hold the same rank. Low-ranking females pass on their low rank to female **offspring.**

Females stay with their troop for their entire lives. They must learn how to get along with others. One way to get along is by grooming. Grooming is a daily event

*Olive baboons play with their family. Just like human children,
young baboons spend lots of time playing.*

Would You Believe?

Baboons spend most of their waking hours traveling and foraging. A troop eats the food in an area and then moves to another feeding range. Often, a water hole lies far away, and baboons need to drink at least every two days. In the dry season, baboons often stop at watering holes two or three times a day. Traveling uses up plenty of daylight hours.

among baboons. It is a waterless bath, ridding fur of dirt, dead skin, and insects. Wild baboons are surprisingly clean.

An olive baboon grooms another member of its troop. Grooming is an important social ritual. It helps create bonds between troop members and keeps the baboons clean.

Males and females begin following different paths by about three years of age. As adults, males must fight other baboons for mates and defend the troop against **predators.** Males roughhouse and wrestle to build strength and develop fighting skills for later life. Three-year-old females show more interest in grooming.

Baboons reach adolescence at four or five years old. Females can produce young at this age. They mate with older, dominant males. At five, males hit a growth spurt. By seven years old, most male baboons weigh twice as much as females. Males reach full maturity when they are between seven and ten years old.

GROWING OLDER

Once females begin having children, they produce an infant every one-and-a-half to two years. By age fifteen, a female might be a mother, grandmother, and great-grandmother. Family ties are strong among females, and a female's relatives usually share the same sleeping site. Younger females within the family babysit younger brothers and sisters. This is good training for later life as a mother.

Females teach the young how to find food. Baboons are omnivores—they

Would You Believe?
Chacma baboons can pull the stingers off scorpions. It is a valuable skill. Scorpions make excellent eating—once the baboon doesn't have to worry about being stung.

eat plants and other animals. They feed on grasses, roots, fruit, seeds, and flowers. They also eat insects, worms, eggs, small birds, and animals such as baby antelopes and small monkeys.

As young adults, males leave the troop to find a new home. This event, called dispersal, is hard on a baboon. It may be the first time the male has been alone. Dispersal is also dangerous. Baboons in a group can fend off attacks by predators. Leopards, hyenas, jackals, cheetahs, and lions are natural enemies of baboons. Single males often become meals for these predators.

When a male finds a new troop, he fights for rank among the other males. Winning battles gives a male a chance to mate, and weaklings are stopped from mating because females want a strong mate. The idea is that strong mates produce strong babies.

SENIORS

Senior citizen baboons do not enjoy a comfortable retirement. As they age, their teeth decay, which makes eating harder. Their joints ache, and traveling with the troop becomes painful. They are often killed by predators.

Males that once held a dominant rank can no longer fight and win. They lose rank and the right to mate

with females. Sometimes they leave the troop to find a new home.

Senior females pass the age when they can produce young. A lucky female has produced many healthy daughters. Her daughters and granddaughters help her survive. They groom her, feed her, and keep the family bonds strong. For a female with few relatives, life becomes lonely. Female baboons need company to be happy.

Baboons have different life spans depending on their species and living conditions. Baboons that live near ample food and few predators live about thirty to forty-five years. Those living in harsh conditions usually die at younger ages.

A hungry lion chases a baboon.

Chapter Three

A Baboon's Day

This is the story of a day in the life of Mila, a two-year-old yellow baboon living in Amboseli National Park in Kenya. Several hundred yellow baboons live in troops there. They have plentiful food and ample water, although the amount of water depends on heavy rains that fall between February and May.

Amboseli gets its name from the Masai people of East Africa. It means "salty dust," and the name is accurate. The area is covered with dry grasslands and dotted with occasional swamps. Needlegrass and star grass dominate Amboseli's plains. Acacia trees, baobabs, and sausage trees provide fruit, leaves, and shelter. Along well-worn trails, more than 900 elephants amble from one water hole to another. Zebras, giraffes, wildebeests, and antelopes graze among the tall grasses.

Mila sleeps on a rocky cliff beside her mother, Mary. The cliff is a safe, protected sleeping site. Mila's infant sister clings to Mary's belly. When she gets a chance, Mila sneaks a drink from her mother's breast. She was **weaned**

many months ago but still likes a sip of milk on occasion.

As the sun rises, Mila climbs down from the cliff. Other juveniles play chase by a cluster of thorny bushes. Mila joins in and races after her friends. A butterfly flitters nearby. It

Yellow baboons rest on the dusty ground in Amboseli National Park in Kenya. Amboseli is a popular tourist destination because of its abundant wildlife and beautiful views of Mount Kilimanjaro.

A yellow baboon forages on the grassy plains of Amboseli National Park.

Would You Believe?
Baboons don't just feed on plants. They eat more meat than any other primate except humans. Meaty meals can include insects, snails, birds, and small mammals.

draws Mila's attention, and she loses interest in the game.

The adults rise and head out to forage. Dominant males lead the group, followed by females and young. Less powerful males bring up the rear. The foragers find prickly pear cactus. Mila's mother strips the spines from the cactus and shares her food with Mila. The group has foraged in this area for several weeks. Today, they will move to find new food supplies.

As they travel, the group munches on flowering acacia and star grass. Mila picks up a clump of zebra dung. Insects under the dung provide needed protein in Mila's diet.

The group arrives at a water hole. A rival troop is already there. The dominant males of Mila's troop screech and show their 5-centimeter-long (2-inch-long) canine teeth as a threat. The rival baboons finish drinking and back away.

Mila approaches the water hole carefully. Baboons do not like to get wet, so they lean over the water from the bank. The troop has traveled a little more than 3 kilometers (almost 2 miles). Mila is tired, hot, and grumpy. A dominant male finds a sprawling baobab tree where the group rests in the shade. Mila curls up next to her mother, who grooms her daughter as she falls asleep.

The adult males lead the troop toward a grove of acacia trees. Along the way, they pass a stand of fever trees. When the bark is cut, these trees ooze gum. The baboons swarm over the trees in search of the gum. It is baboon candy—sweet and tasty.

A leopard hides behind a clump of tall grass nearby. As the wind shifts, the male baboons pick up the leopard's scent and shriek a warning. The females and young scurry into the fever trees. Mila shakes with fear. Even a two-year-old baboon recognizes danger.

The leopard may be larger, but a group of angry baboon males can defeat a leopard. The leopard slinks away, and the troop heads toward its new sleeping site.

It has been a long day for Mila. As the sun sets, she climbs into an acacia tree beside her mother. She squats on a branch and yawns. Like human children, Mila snuggles down for a welcome night's sleep.

This leopard is unlikely to successfully kill a baboon. Male baboons will fiercely counterattack a predator to protect the troop. Their threatening gestures and aggressive vocalizations are usually enough to confuse a predator and send it on its way.

Chapter Four

The Baboon Family Tree

True baboons are land monkeys. They spend their days foraging for food on open ground. They are highly intelligent, adaptable creatures that adjust to most habitats. Most baboons grow to be 60 to 75 centimeters (24 to 30 in) from head to toe. Their tails are nearly equal in length to their height. Baboon males weigh about twice as much as females. Baboon species include Chacma, Hamadryas, olive, western, and yellow baboons.

Baboons move rapidly on all fours, much like galloping horses. They can walk upright for short distances. Baboons have agile hands with opposing thumbs, like humans. They can peel hulls off seeds using their hands or teeth.

Chacma baboons have dark fur and close-set eyes under a jutting brow. Their long muzzles make their faces look a little

Would You Believe?
Baboons can pull up 150 leaves of grass in a minute.

Though baboons can walk upright for short distances, they usually walk or run on all fours.

like the faces of dogs. Chacma baboons live in southern Africa, usually in savannas, in woodlands, or near scrub acacias. Chacma baboons that live near the coast sometimes eat crabs, mussels, and worms.

Western baboons sport reddish-brown fur. They live in evergreen and gallery forests and woodland savannah, preferring woodlands to open plains. Western baboons are thinner than their Chacma relatives, weighing in at 11 to 27 kilograms (25 to 60 lbs) as adults. They choose palm or kapok trees for sleeping sites and travel in troops of up to 200 individuals. The smallest of the baboons, western baboons are found in Gambia, Guinea, Senegal, and Sierra Leone.

BABOON SPECIES

	Height	Tail Length	Average Weight
Chacma	71–81 cm (28–32 in)	58–64 cm (23–25 in)	Male: 20–34 kg, Female: 17 kg (M: 45–75 lbs, F: 37 lbs)
Hamadryas	76 cm (30 in)	56 cm (22 in)	M: 21 kg, F: 12 kg (M: 47 lbs, F: 27 lbs)
Olive	58–74 cm (23–29 in)	43–53 cm (17–21 in)	M: 23–45 kg, F: 15 kg (M: 50–100 lbs, F: 32 lbs)
Western	69 cm (27 in)	56 cm (22 in)	M: 23–27 kg, F: 11–14 kg (M: 50–60 lbs, F: 25–30 lbs)
Yellow	61–69 cm (24–27 in)	38–56 cm (15–22 in)	M: 25 kg, F: 12 kg (M: 55 lbs, F: 27 lbs)

Hamadryas baboons live in Ethiopia, Egypt, Saudi Arabia, Somalia, Sudan, and Yemen. They are the only nonhuman **primates** living in Arabia. Hamadryas baboons prefer to live in rocky deserts and semiarid deserts with grass. These baboons look like other

Would You Believe?
Hamadryas baboons are the only baboons considered an endangered species.

Hamadryas baboons were sacred animals in ancient Egypt. They were a symbol of the god Thoth who was considered the inventor of writing.

baboons on a bad hair day. Their coat is gray-brown and extremely fluffy.

Olive baboons live in **equatorial** Africa. They are also dog-faced baboons and are heavier than most species. Olive males weigh up to about 45 kilograms (100 lbs), while females are usually no more than 15 kilograms (32 lbs) or so. Olive baboons eat most anything and live most anywhere—woodlands, grasslands, or semideserts.

Male olive baboons have a large mane of hair on their head and shoulders.

Yellow baboons also live in equatorial Africa and along Africa's eastern coast. Yellow baboons are usually smaller than their olive cousins. Their fur is lighter in color, and they have less fur than olive baboons. Like most baboons, they communicate using clicks, grunts, howls, and screeches. They smack and curl their lips. They also stare, show their teeth, and raise their eyebrows—much like angry humans.

GELADAS, DRILLS, AND MANDRILLS

Although they are sometimes mistaken for baboons, mandrills, and drills are only distant relatives of the baboon while geladas are closer to baboons but still different. Geladas, called bleeding heart baboons, live in Ethiopia. They get their nickname from the bald, red, heart-shaped patches on the chests of males. Geladas have long, brown fur and are roughly the same size as savanna baboons. They also forage for grass, roots, bulbs, leaves, and fruits, and they choose rocky cliffs for sleeping sites. About 50,000 to 60,000 geladas live in the wild.

Mandrills and drills are colorful primates. They are forest-dwellers, living in western central Africa, Cameroon, Gabon, and Congo. They are endangered in the wild. Most of the population live in zoos around the world. Mandrills

are noted for their vivid-red snouts with blue and white side stripes. They have bright blue or lilac rumps and yellow ruffs around their necks. A mandrill's size, shape, and diet resemble those of baboons, but mandrills and drills prefer to live in rain forests rather than open savannas.

A female mandrill and her baby sit in a tree.

Chapter Five

The Past, The Present, and The Future

In ancient Egypt, the baboon was sacred. Many were kept as pets, and tomb murals show baboons on leashes or playing with family members. Sadly, baboons are no longer as plentiful as they once were in Egypt. Many have been killed off over time.

Conservation groups keep close watch over Hamadryas and western baboon populations. There are fewer of these baboons than Chacma, olive, or yellow baboons.

Most baboon species are neither endangered nor threatened in the wild. Unlike elephants with ivory tusks and leopards with beautiful fur, baboons do not have parts that are easily sold. Yet, poaching continues. Customs agents in the Netherlands found suitcases filled with 2,000 baboon noses. The use for these noses was uncertain. They could have been

Would You Believe?
The Samburu people of Kenya have a deep respect for baboons. According to legend, some Samburu children went to live among baboons during a long period of drought. These children survived, while many who remained with the tribe died. The Samburu know that baboons can find water even in the driest times.

Baboons crowd together in a cage.

used as food or for making medicine.

In Tanzania, poachers trap baboons in crude cages. They sell live baboons for about twelve dollars each to laboratories that experiment on the animals. Agencies trying to stop trade in baboons and baboon parts fight an uphill battle. It is difficult to monitor baboon troops that move constantly over so much territory.

When a mother baboon dies or is trapped, her infant baboon becomes an orphan. Sometimes, female relatives will adopt the orphan. If not, **rehabilitation** centers provide homes for orphaned baboons. Volunteers feed and play with the young. The baboons live with other

Adult baboons with a baby at a zoo in Munich, Germany.

orphans and form small troops. The goal is to eventually return the baboons to the wild.

The baboons' ability to adjust to changing environments is both a blessing and a bother. No matter where the baboons go, they quickly find new things to eat, including garbage, crops, and gardens. As people move into baboon territories, they discover that baboons can become destructive pests. In farm regions, baboons are often shot or trapped when they raid crops.

One answer to saving species lies in zoo programs. A fairly large baboon population lives in zoos throughout the world. Zoos trade animals for breeding purposes under what is called a species survival plan. For baboons, the trading process is like dispersal, the natural movement of adult males from troop to troop.

Hamadryas and western baboons, geladas, drills, and mandrills are all covered under zoo species survival plans. Drills and mandrills have larger populations in captivity than in the wild. Captive breeding programs are saving these brilliant, colorful primates from becoming extinct. Humans must learn to live side by side with baboon troops. If not, extinction may become the future for all baboon species.

Glossary

adolescents (ad-uh-LESS-uhnts) individuals in a preadult stage of life; teenagers

dominant (DOM-uh-nuhnt) the strongest or most powerful in a group

equatorial (ek-wuh-TOR-ee-uhl) lying along the equator

foraging (FOR-uhj-ing) searching for food

juvenile (JOO-vuh-nile) a young, immature animal

muzzle (MUHZ-uhl) the nose, mouth and jaw of an animal

offspring (OFF-spring) the young of an animal or human

predators (PRED-uh-turz) animals that hunt other animals for food

primates (PRY-mates) mammals in the group that includes monkeys, apes, lemurs, and humans

rehabilitation (ree-uh-bil-ih-TAY-shun) a program for restoring an individual to normal life

savanna (suh-VAN-uh) a flat, grassy plain

species (SPEE-sheez) a group of animals that share certain characteristics

troop (TROOP) a group of animals that live together

vermin (VUR-min) animals that are pests, such as mice and rats

weaned (WEEND) gave up something gradually

For More Information

Watch It

Wild Animal Kingdom: Mountain Gorillas, Snow Monkeys, and Baboons,
VHS (Chicago: Questar, 1999)

Read It

Barrett, Louise. *Baboons.* New York: Dorling Kindersley Publishing,
2001.

Buller, Jon, and Susan Schade. *Bungee Baboon Rescue.* New York:
Scholastic, 2002.

Horak, Steven A. *Baboons and Other Old World Monkeys.* Chicago:
World Book, 2002.

Look It Up

Visit our home page for lots of links about baboons:
http://www.childsworld.com/links

Note to Parents, Teachers, and Librarians: We routinely verify our Web
links to make sure they are safe, active sites—so encourage your
readers to check them out!

The Animal Kingdom
Where Do Baboons Fit In?

Kingdom: Animal

Phylum: Chordates (animals with backbones)

Class: Mammalia (animals that feed their young milk)

Order: Primates

Family: Cercopithecidae

Genus: *Papio*

Species:
P. anubis (olive)

P. cynocephalus (yellow)

P. hamadryas (Hamadryas)

P. papio (western)

P. ursinus (Chacma)

Index

About the Author

Sophie Lockwood is a former teacher and a longtime writer. She writes textbooks, newspaper articles, and magazine articles. Sophie enjoys writing about animals and their habits. The most interesting part of her research, Sophie says, is learning how scientists apply their knowledge to save endangered species. She lives with her husband in the foothills of the Blue Ridge Mountains.